The Essential Blueprint for Building a Successful Online Business from Scratch

Topics:

- Business Startups
- Online Entrepreneurship
- Digital Marketing
- E-commerce

Audience:
- Aspiring Entrepreneurs
- Small Business Owners
- Digital Marketers
- Startups Founders

Purpose:
- How-to Guides
- Business Strategy
- Entrepreneurial Advice
- Success Planning

Industry:
- Technology
- Retail
- Services
- Online Commerce

Content:
- Educational
- Instructional
- Resourceful
- Practical Tips

Stage of business:
- Startup
- Growth
- Planning
- Launch

Navigating the Startup Journey: Essential Steps for Building a Successful Business from Scratch

Starting a business can be an exhilarating and daunting journey. From refining your idea to scaling your operations, the path to success is filled with critical steps that can make or break your venture. This guide outlines essential steps to help you launch and grow a successful startup.

1. Define Your Business Idea

Before diving into the logistics, clearly define your business idea. What problem does it solve? Who is your target audience? Conduct thorough market research to validate your concept and ensure there is demand. Consider factors like market size, competition, and customer needs.

2. Develop a Business Plan

A well-structured business plan serves as a roadmap for your startup. It should include:

- Executive Summary: A snapshot of your business and its goals.
- Market Analysis: Insights into industry trends and target market.
- Business Model: How you will generate revenue.
- Marketing Strategy: Plans for reaching and attracting customers.
- Financial Projections: Estimated costs, revenue, and profitability.
- Operations Plan: Details on day-to-day operations and management.

3. Secure Funding

Determine how much capital you need and explore funding options. This could include personal savings, loans, venture capital, angel investors, or crowdfunding. Prepare a solid pitch and financial projections to attract investors.

4. Register Your Business

Choose a suitable business structure (e.g., sole proprietorship, partnership, LLC, corporation) and register your business name. Ensure you comply with local regulations and obtain necessary licenses or permits.

5. Build Your Brand

Create a strong brand identity that resonates with your target audience. This includes designing a memorable logo, crafting a compelling value proposition, and developing a consistent brand voice. Your brand should reflect your business values and mission.

6. Set Up Your Online Presence

In today's digital age, having an online presence is crucial. Develop a professional website, and optimize it for search engines (SEO). Utilize social media platforms to connect with your audience and drive traffic to your site. Consider using online tools for customer engagement and marketing.

7. Develop Your Product or Service

Focus on creating a high-quality product or service that meets customer needs. Iterate based on feedback and ensure it stands out from competitors. Test your product thoroughly before launch to address any issues.

8. Launch Your Startup

Prepare for a successful launch by building anticipation through marketing and public relations efforts. Host launch events, engage with influencers, and use social media to generate buzz. Monitor initial responses and adjust your strategy as needed.

9. Monitor and Adapt

Post-launch, continuously track your performance using key metrics and analytics. Be prepared to adapt your strategies based on customer feedback and market trends. Regularly review your business plan and make necessary adjustments to stay on course.

10. Focus on Growth

As your business stabilizes, shift your focus to growth. Explore new markets, enhance your product offerings, and invest in marketing and innovation. Building a strong team and fostering a positive company culture will also contribute to long-term success.

Starting a business requires careful planning, dedication, and adaptability. By following these essential steps, you can navigate the complexities of launching a startup and increase your chances of building a successful and sustainable business. Remember, perseverance and a willingness to learn from challenges are key to thriving in the entrepreneurial world.

Embracing Online Entrepreneurship: A Guide to Building a Thriving Digital Business

In today's digital age, online entrepreneurship offers

unparalleled opportunities to create and scale businesses. From launching e-commerce stores to offering digital services, the online realm provides a vast playground for innovative entrepreneurs. Here's a comprehensive guide to help you navigate the world of online entrepreneurship and build a successful digital business.

1. Identify Your Niche

Success in online entrepreneurship often begins with identifying a niche market. Consider your passions, skills, and areas where you can offer unique value. Conduct market research to understand customer needs, assess competition, and discover opportunities. A well-defined niche helps you target your audience more effectively and stand out in a crowded marketplace.

2. Create a Solid Business Plan

A business plan is crucial for outlining your online business strategy. It should include:

- Business Concept: Define your value proposition and how you plan to deliver it online.
- Market Analysis: Research your target audience, competitors, and industry trends.
- Revenue Model: Determine how you will generate income, whether through sales, subscriptions, or ads.
- Marketing Strategy: Plan how to attract and retain customers using digital channels.
- Financial Projections: Estimate startup costs, ongoing expenses, and revenue forecasts.

3. Build Your Online Presence

Your online presence is the cornerstone of your business. Start with a professional website that is user-friendly, mobile-responsive, and optimized for search engines (SEO). Invest in high-quality visuals and content that clearly communicate your brand message and offerings.

4. Leverage Digital Marketing

Effective digital marketing is key to driving traffic and sales. Utilize various strategies, such as:

- Content Marketing: Create valuable content to engage your audience and build trust.
- Social Media: Use platforms like Facebook, Instagram, and LinkedIn to connect with your audience and promote your brand.
- Email Marketing: Build an email list and send targeted campaigns to nurture leads and drive conversions.
- Paid Advertising: Invest in PPC, display ads, or social media ads to reach a broader audience and boost visibility.

5. Optimize for E-commerce

If you're running an online store, focus on optimizing the e-commerce experience. Ensure your website is easy to navigate, offers secure payment options, and provides excellent customer service. Implement strategies like abandoned cart recovery and personalized recommendations to enhance the shopping experience.

6. Develop a Content Strategy

Content is vital for attracting and retaining customers. Develop a content strategy that includes blog posts, videos, infographics, and other formats that resonate with your audience. Consistent, high-quality content helps build your brand's authority and drives organic traffic to your website.

7. Monitor Analytics and Adapt

Regularly track your business performance using analytics tools. Monitor key metrics such as website traffic, conversion rates, and customer behavior. Use these insights to refine your strategies, optimize your marketing efforts, and improve overall performance.

8. Build an Engaged Community

Fostering an engaged online community can drive brand loyalty and advocacy. Encourage interactions through social media, forums, or user-generated content. Listen to customer feedback and use it to enhance your products and services.

9. Stay Current with Trends

The digital landscape is constantly evolving. Stay informed about the latest trends, tools, and technologies in online entrepreneurship. Adapt your strategies to leverage new opportunities and remain competitive in the dynamic online market.

10. Focus on Scalability

Plan for growth from the start. Build systems and processes that can scale as your business expands. Invest in automation tools and scalable solutions to manage increased traffic and operations efficiently.

Online entrepreneurship presents exciting possibilities for those willing to embrace the digital world. By following these steps and staying adaptable, you can build a successful online business that thrives in today's interconnected marketplace. With a clear strategy, effective marketing, and a focus on customer experience, you can turn your online entrepreneurial dreams into reality.

Mastering Digital Marketing: Strategies for Success in the Modern Landscapes

Digital marketing has revolutionized the way businesses connect with their audiences, offering unparalleled opportunities to drive growth and engagement. In a landscape where online presence is crucial, understanding and implementing effective digital marketing strategies can set your business apart. This guide explores key digital marketing techniques to help you craft a successful online strategy.

1. Understand Your Audience

The foundation of any successful digital marketing campaign is a deep understanding of your target audience. Use tools like Google Analytics, social media insights, and customer surveys to gather data on demographics, interests, and online behavior. Create detailed buyer personas to tailor your marketing efforts to the specific needs and preferences of your audience.

2. Develop a Content Marketing Strategy

Content marketing is central to attracting and engaging your audience. A well-developed content strategy includes:

- Content Creation: Produce high-quality, valuable content such as blog posts, videos,

infographics, and podcasts that address your audience's pain points and interests.
- Content Distribution: Use various channels like your website, social media, and email newsletters to distribute your content.
- Content Calendar: Plan and schedule content to maintain consistency and ensure a steady flow of fresh material.

3. Optimize for Search Engines (SEO)

Search engine optimization (SEO) enhances your online visibility by improving your website's ranking on search engine results pages (SERPs). Focus on:

- Keyword Research: Identify and use relevant keywords that your audience is searching for.
- On-Page SEO: Optimize elements like title tags, meta descriptions, headers, and content for targeted keywords.
- Off-Page SEO: Build backlinks from reputable sites to boost your website's authority.
- Technical SEO: Ensure your website's technical aspects, like site speed and mobile-friendliness, are optimized for search engines.

4. Leverage Social Media Marketing

Social media platforms are powerful tools for brand awareness and customer engagement. Key strategies include:

- Platform Selection: Choose platforms that align with your audience demographics and business goals.
- Content Sharing: Post engaging content, interact with followers, and use features like stories and

live videos to connect with your audience.
- Paid Advertising: Utilize targeted ads to reach specific audiences and drive traffic to your website.

5. Invest in Pay-Per-Click (PPC) Advertising

PPC advertising, including Google Ads and social media ads, allows you to target specific audiences and achieve immediate visibility. Focus on:

- Ad Creation: Develop compelling ad copy and visuals that drive clicks and conversions.

- Keyword Targeting: Choose relevant keywords to ensure your ads reach the right audience.
- Budget Management: Set and manage your ad budget to maximize ROI while controlling costs.

6. Utilize Email Marketing

Email marketing remains one of the most effective channels for nurturing leads and driving conversions. Key tactics include:

- Segmentation: Divide your email list into segments based on behavior, preferences, and

demographics to deliver personalized content.
- Automation: Use automated email sequences for welcome messages, follow-ups, and abandoned cart reminders.
- A/B Testing: Test different subject lines, content, and calls to action to optimize email performance.

7. Monitor and Analyze Performance

Regularly tracking and analyzing your digital marketing efforts is essential for continuous improvement. Use tools like

Google Analytics, social media insights, and email analytics to monitor:

- Key Metrics: Track metrics such as website traffic, conversion rates, click-through rates, and engagement levels.
- Performance Trends: Identify patterns and trends to refine your strategies and improve results.

8. Embrace Mobile Marketing

With the increasing use of mobile devices, optimizing your digital marketing for mobile users is crucial. Ensure your website is mobile-friendly, create mobile-optimized ads, and consider SMS marketing to reach users on their smartphones.

9. Focus on Customer Experience

Enhancing the customer experience can drive loyalty and positive word-of-mouth. Provide seamless interactions across all touchpoints, from user-friendly website navigation to responsive customer service.

10. Stay Updated with Trends

The digital marketing landscape is constantly evolving. Stay informed about emerging trends, tools, and technologies to keep your strategies relevant and effective. Participate in industry webinars, read marketing blogs, and follow thought leaders to stay ahead of the curve.

Digital marketing offers a wealth of opportunities for businesses to engage with their audience and achieve growth. By understanding your audience, leveraging diverse marketing strategies, and continuously optimizing your efforts, you can build a robust digital presence that drives success in today's competitive landscape.

the E-Commerce Landscape: Key Strategies for Building a Successful Online Store

E-commerce has transformed the retail industry, allowing businesses to reach global audiences and operate 24/7. With the rise of online shopping, creating a successful e-commerce store requires more than just listing products online. This guide explores essential strategies for building and managing a thriving e-commerce business.

1. Choose the Right E-Commerce Platform

Selecting the right e-commerce platform is crucial for your store's success. Consider factors such as ease of use, scalability, customization options, and integration capabilities. Popular platforms include:

- Shopify: Known for its user-friendly interface and extensive app ecosystem.

- WooCommerce: A flexible plugin for WordPress users, offering customizable features.
- Magento: A powerful platform for larger businesses needing advanced features and scalability.
- BigCommerce: Ideal for businesses seeking a comprehensive solution with built-in tools.

2. Design a User-Friendly Website

Your e-commerce website should provide a seamless shopping experience. Focus on:

- Navigation: Ensure intuitive and easy-to-use menus and search functionality.
- Responsive Design: Optimize for mobile devices to accommodate the growing number of mobile shoppers.
- Product Pages: Create detailed product descriptions, high-quality images, and clear pricing information. Incorporate customer reviews and ratings to build trust.

3. Implement Effective SEO Strategies

Search engine optimization (SEO) helps drive organic traffic to your e-commerce site. Key SEO tactics include:

- Keyword Research: Identify relevant keywords for your product pages and content.
- On-Page SEO: Optimize product titles, meta descriptions, and URLs with target keywords.
- Content Marketing: Create valuable content such as blog posts, buying guides, and product comparisons to attract and engage potential customers.
- Technical SEO: Ensure your site's loading speed, mobile-friendliness, and site

structure are optimized for search engines.

4. Optimize for Conversion

Converting visitors into customers is the ultimate goal of any e-commerce store. Enhance your conversion rate by:

- Clear Call-to-Actions (CTAs): Use prominent and persuasive CTAs on product pages and throughout the checkout process.
- Simplified Checkout: Reduce friction by offering guest checkout options, multiple payment

methods, and a streamlined process.
- Trust Signals: Display security badges, customer reviews, and return policies to build trust and reduce cart abandonment.

5. Develop a Robust Digital Marketing Strategy

Attracting and retaining customers requires a well-rounded digital marketing approach. Consider:

- Social Media Marketing: Promote your products through targeted ads and engaging content on platforms like

Facebook, Instagram, and Pinterest.
- Email Marketing: Build an email list and send personalized campaigns, promotions, and abandoned cart reminders.
- Pay-Per-Click (PPC) Advertising: Use platforms like Google Ads and social media ads to drive traffic and increase sales.

6. Focus on Customer Service

Exceptional customer service is key to building long-term relationships and driving repeat business. Provide:

- Responsive Support: Offer multiple channels for customer support, such as live chat, email, and phone.
- Easy Returns: Implement a straightforward return and exchange process to enhance customer satisfaction.
- Personalization: Use data to personalize customer interactions and recommendations based on purchase history and browsing behavior.

7. Analyze and Optimize Performance

Regularly monitor and analyze your e-commerce store's performance to identify areas for improvement. Track key metrics such as:

- Sales Data: Analyze sales trends, average order value, and conversion rates.
- Customer Behavior: Use tools like Google Analytics to understand how visitors interact with your site.
- Marketing Effectiveness: Evaluate the performance of your marketing campaigns and adjust strategies based on ROI.

8. Embrace Technology and Automation

Leverage technology to streamline operations and enhance efficiency. Consider:

- Inventory Management: Use inventory management systems to keep track of stock levels and automate reordering.
- Customer Relationship Management (CRM): Implement CRM tools to manage customer interactions and track sales leads.
- Automation Tools: Utilize marketing automation for email

campaigns, social media posts, and customer segmentation.

9. Ensure Security and Compliance

Protecting customer data and complying with regulations is critical for maintaining trust. Focus on:

- Secure Transactions: Use SSL certificates to encrypt data and ensure secure payment processing.
- Data Privacy: Comply with regulations like GDPR and CCPA

to protect customer information and privacy.
- Fraud Prevention: Implement measures to detect and prevent fraudulent transactions.

10. Stay Current with E-Commerce Trends

The e-commerce landscape is continually evolving. Stay updated with trends such as:

- Mobile Commerce: Optimize for mobile shopping experiences and consider developing a mobile app.
- Artificial Intelligence: Explore AI tools for personalized

recommendations and customer service.

- Sustainability: Embrace eco-friendly practices and communicate your commitment to sustainability to attract environmentally conscious consumers.

Building a successful e-commerce store involves careful planning, strategic execution, and continuous optimization. By selecting the right platform, designing a user-friendly website, and implementing effective marketing and customer service strategies, you can create a thriving online business that stands out in the competitive digital marketplace. Stay adaptable and informed to keep pace with industry trends and drive long-term success.

Audience

Aspiring Entrepreneurship in Online Business: Navigating the Digital Frontier

In today's digital age, aspiring entrepreneurs have unprecedented opportunities to build and grow businesses online.

The internet has transformed traditional business models, making it possible for individuals to launch ventures with relatively low startup costs and reach global audiences. However, while the digital landscape offers immense potential, it also presents unique challenges. Here's a closer look at what aspiring online entrepreneurs need to consider to navigate this dynamic field successfully.

1. Identifying a Niche

Success in online business often begins with identifying a niche market. A well-defined niche helps differentiate a business from competitors and targets specific customer needs. Aspiring entrepreneurs should conduct thorough market research to uncover underserved areas or emerging trends. Tools like Google Trends, social media analytics, and keyword research can provide valuable insights into consumer behavior and preferences.

2. Building a Strong Online Presence

Establishing a robust online presence is crucial. This includes creating a professional website that effectively communicates your brand's value proposition. User experience (UX) and search engine optimization (SEO) are critical components. A well-designed website that is easy to navigate and optimized for search engines can significantly enhance visibility and attract potential customers.

3. Leveraging Social Media

Social media platforms are powerful tools for building brand awareness and engaging with customers. Each platform—whether Facebook, Instagram, Twitter, or LinkedIn—offers unique ways to connect with audiences. Aspiring entrepreneurs should develop a social media strategy that aligns with their brand identity and target audience. Consistent, high-quality content and active engagement can foster a loyal online community.

4. Utilizing E-Commerce Tools

For those looking to sell products or services online, e-commerce tools are indispensable. Platforms like Shopify, WooCommerce, and BigCommerce offer user-friendly solutions for setting up online stores, managing inventory, and processing payments. Additionally, integrating analytics tools can help track sales performance and customer behavior, enabling data-driven decision-making.

5. Embracing Digital Marketing

Digital marketing encompasses various strategies to promote an online business, including content marketing, email marketing, pay-per-click advertising, and influencer partnerships. A well-rounded digital marketing plan can drive traffic to your website, generate leads, and increase conversions. Aspiring entrepreneurs should stay updated on digital marketing trends and continuously optimize their campaigns for better results.

6. Understanding Legal and Regulatory Requirements

Operating an online business involves navigating legal and regulatory requirements. These can include data protection laws, intellectual property rights, and online business licenses. Entrepreneurs must ensure they comply with relevant regulations to avoid legal issues and build trust with their customers.

7. Managing Finances and Budgeting

Effective financial management is crucial for any business. Aspiring online entrepreneurs should create a detailed business plan and budget that outlines startup costs, operating expenses, and revenue projections. Utilizing financial management tools and software can help track expenses, manage cash flow, and make informed financial decisions.

8. Adapting to Change

The online business landscape is continually evolving, with new technologies and trends emerging regularly. Aspiring entrepreneurs need to be adaptable and open to change. Staying informed about industry developments and being willing to pivot or innovate can help sustain long-term success.

9. Building a Network

Networking is essential for gaining insights, opportunities, and support. Engaging with other entrepreneurs, industry experts, and potential customers can provide valuable feedback and open doors to collaborations or partnerships. Online forums, social media groups, and industry events are excellent places to build connections.

10. Maintaining Persistence and Resilience

The journey of online entrepreneurship can be challenging, with setbacks and obstacles along the way. Persistence and resilience are key traits for overcoming difficulties and achieving long-term success. Learning from failures, continuously improving, and staying motivated can help aspiring entrepreneurs navigate the ups and downs of the online business world.

Aspiring entrepreneurs in the online business arena have the advantage of leveraging digital tools and platforms to reach a global audience and scale their ventures. By focusing on niche identification, building a strong online presence, utilizing digital marketing, and staying adaptable, they can set themselves up for success. Embracing these strategies and maintaining resilience in the face of challenges will pave the way for a thriving online business venture.

The Journey of a Small Business Owner: Navigating Challenges and Seizing Opportunities

Small business owners play a crucial role in the economy, driving innovation, creating jobs, and fostering community growth. However, the path to success in small business ownership is often filled with both rewards and challenges. Understanding these dynamics is essential for anyone looking to thrive as a small business owner.

1. Embracing the Entrepreneurial Spirit

At the heart of every small business is an entrepreneurial spirit—an individual with a vision and the drive to turn it into reality. Small business owners must be passionate about their product or service and willing to put in the hard work required to succeed. This dedication often involves long hours, a willingness to take risks, and a commitment to continuous learning.

2. Developing a Solid Business Plan

A well-crafted business plan serves as a roadmap for a small business. It outlines the business's goals, target market, competitive landscape, and financial projections. This plan not only helps in securing funding but also guides strategic decisions and helps track progress. Regularly revisiting and updating the business plan ensures it remains relevant and aligned with evolving goals.

3. Managing Finances Wisely

Financial management is a cornerstone of small business success. Owners must keep a close eye on cash flow, manage expenses, and plan for taxes. Using accounting software or consulting with a financial advisor can simplify these tasks and provide valuable insights into the business's financial health. Proper budgeting and financial planning are essential for maintaining stability and fueling growth.

4. Building a Strong Brand

Creating a strong brand identity is crucial for standing out in a competitive market. This includes developing a compelling brand message, designing a memorable logo, and maintaining consistent branding across all channels. A strong brand helps build customer trust and loyalty, making it easier to attract and retain clients.

5. Focusing on Customer Experience

Exceptional customer service can set a small business apart from its competitors. Small business owners should prioritize creating positive customer experiences, addressing concerns promptly, and soliciting feedback. Happy customers are more likely to become repeat clients and refer others, which can drive growth through word-of-mouth.

6. Leveraging Technology

Technology can be a powerful ally for small business owners. From customer relationship management (CRM) systems and e-commerce platforms to social media marketing and data analytics, leveraging the right tools can enhance efficiency, expand reach, and provide valuable insights. Staying updated on technological advancements helps small businesses remain competitive and agile.

7. Navigating Regulatory Requirements

Compliance with local, state, and federal regulations is a critical aspect of running a small business. This includes understanding tax obligations, labor laws, health and safety standards, and industry-specific regulations. Small business owners must stay informed about relevant legal requirements to avoid penalties and ensure smooth operations.

8. Developing a Marketing Strategy

Effective marketing is key to driving visibility and attracting customers. Small business owners should develop a comprehensive marketing strategy that includes online and offline tactics. This might involve social media campaigns, content marketing, email newsletters, and local advertising. Measuring the effectiveness of marketing efforts allows for adjustments and optimization.

9. Building a Support Network

Having a support network can be invaluable for small business owners. Connecting with other entrepreneurs, industry professionals, and local business organizations can provide advice, resources, and networking opportunities. Mentorship from experienced business owners can also offer guidance and encouragement.

10. Adapting and Innovating

Flexibility and innovation are essential traits for small business owners. The ability to adapt to market changes, customer preferences, and emerging trends can significantly impact a business's success. Regularly assessing the business environment and being open to new ideas or improvements can help maintain relevance and drive growth.

Small business ownership is a journey marked by both challenges and opportunities. By embracing the entrepreneurial spirit, managing finances wisely, building a strong brand, and focusing on customer experience, small business owners can create a solid foundation for success. Leveraging technology, staying compliant with regulations, and continuously innovating are also crucial for thriving in a competitive landscape. With dedication and strategic planning, small business owners can navigate their path to success and make a meaningful impact on their communities.

The Role and Evolution of Digital Marketers in the Modern Business Landscape

Digital marketers are pivotal in today's business world, where online presence and digital engagement are crucial for success. Their role has evolved significantly with technological advancements and shifting consumer behaviors, making them essential for driving growth and brand visibility in the digital age.

1. Understanding the Digital Marketing Landscape

Digital marketing encompasses various strategies to promote products and services online. This includes search engine optimization (SEO), content marketing, social media marketing, email marketing, and pay-per-click (PPC) advertising. Digital marketers utilize these tools to build brand awareness, engage audiences, and drive conversions.

2. Crafting Data-Driven Strategies

A key responsibility of digital marketers is to develop data-driven strategies. By analyzing data from web analytics, social media metrics, and customer interactions, they can gain insights into consumer behavior and campaign performance. This data allows for the optimization of marketing efforts and the refinement of strategies to achieve better results.

3. Mastering Content Creation and Management

Content is a cornerstone of digital marketing. Marketers must create and manage high-quality content that resonates with their target audience. This involves writing compelling blog posts, crafting engaging social media updates, and producing multimedia content like videos and infographics. Effective content not only attracts and retains customers but also enhances brand credibility.

4. Leveraging Social Media Platforms

Social media platforms are integral to modern marketing strategies. Digital marketers must be adept at using platforms such as Facebook, Instagram, Twitter, and LinkedIn to engage with audiences, promote content, and drive traffic to websites. Each platform has its nuances, and marketers need to tailor their approach to fit the platform's audience and capabilities.

5. Utilizing SEO and SEM

Search engine optimization (SEO) and search engine marketing (SEM) are essential for increasing online visibility. SEO focuses on improving a website's organic search rankings through keyword optimization, on-page and off-page strategies, and technical enhancements. SEM, including paid search ads, helps drive targeted traffic quickly. Digital marketers must balance both approaches to maximize search engine presence.

6. Implementing Email Marketing Campaigns

Email marketing remains a powerful tool for nurturing leads and maintaining customer relationships. Digital marketers design and execute email campaigns to deliver personalized content, promotions, and updates. Successful email marketing involves segmenting audiences, crafting engaging messages, and analyzing open and click-through rates to refine strategies.

7. Staying Current with Trends and Technologies

The digital marketing landscape is constantly evolving with new trends and technologies. Marketers must stay informed about emerging tools, platforms, and best practices. This includes understanding developments in artificial intelligence, automation, and emerging social media trends. Keeping up with these changes helps marketers stay competitive and innovative.

8. Measuring and Analyzing Performance

Effective digital marketing requires ongoing measurement and analysis. Marketers use various tools and metrics to track campaign performance, including website traffic, conversion rates, and return on investment (ROI). Regularly analyzing this data allows for the assessment of what's working, what needs improvement, and how to allocate resources effectively.

9. Fostering Customer Engagement

Engaging with customers is crucial for building brand loyalty and driving conversions. Digital marketers use various tactics to foster engagement, such as interactive content, social media interactions, and personalized messaging. Building strong relationships with customers helps enhance brand reputation and encourages repeat business.

10. Adapting to Regulatory Changes

Digital marketers must navigate regulatory requirements related to data privacy and online advertising. Compliance with regulations such as GDPR (General Data Protection Regulation) and CCPA (California Consumer Privacy Act) is essential for maintaining customer trust and avoiding legal issues. Staying informed about regulatory changes helps ensure marketing practices are ethical and compliant.

Digital marketers play a vital role in shaping how brands connect with their audiences and drive growth in the digital world. By leveraging data, mastering content creation, utilizing SEO and SEM, and staying current with industry trends, they create effective strategies that enhance brand visibility and engagement. As the digital landscape continues to evolve, digital marketers must remain adaptable and innovative to succeed in an increasingly competitive environment.

The Journey of Startup Founders: Navigating Innovation and Growth

Startup founders are the visionaries driving the next wave of innovation and entrepreneurship. Their journey is marked by passion, perseverance, and the relentless pursuit of transforming ideas into successful ventures. Understanding the role and challenges of startup founders provides insight into the entrepreneurial spirit that fuels today's dynamic business landscape.

1. The Vision Behind the Startup

At the heart of every startup is a founder with a compelling vision. This vision often stems from a desire to solve a problem, address a market gap, or revolutionize an existing industry. Startup founders are driven by a deep sense of purpose and a commitment to bringing their ideas to life. Crafting a clear and impactful vision is essential for guiding the startup's direction and inspiring the team.

2. Building the Foundation

The initial stages of a startup involve laying a strong foundation. This includes developing a business plan, defining the value proposition, and setting clear goals. Founders must also build a prototype or minimum viable product (MVP) to test their concept and gather feedback. Establishing a solid business model and identifying target customers are critical steps in positioning the startup for success.

3. Assembling a Talented Team

A startup's success is often tied to the strength of its team. Founders must attract and retain talented individuals who share their vision and bring diverse skills to the table. Building a cohesive and motivated team involves effective recruitment, fostering a positive culture, and providing opportunities for growth and development. A strong team can drive innovation, execute the business plan, and navigate challenges together.

4. Securing Funding

Funding is a crucial aspect of growing a startup. Founders need to explore various financing options, including bootstrapping, venture capital, angel investors, and crowdfunding. Each option has its pros and cons, and founders must choose the one that aligns with their goals and business stage. Pitching to investors requires a compelling narrative, a solid business plan, and a clear demonstration of the startup's potential.

5. Navigating Challenges and Uncertainty

The journey of a startup founder is often fraught with challenges and uncertainties. From market competition and financial constraints to operational hurdles and regulatory issues, founders must be resilient and adaptable. Embracing a problem-solving mindset, learning from failures, and continuously iterating the business model are essential for overcoming obstacles and achieving long-term success.

6. Fostering Innovation

Innovation is at the core of every successful startup. Founders must foster a culture of creativity and experimentation, encouraging the team to explore new ideas and approaches. Staying ahead of industry trends and leveraging emerging technologies can provide a competitive edge and drive continuous improvement. Innovation helps startups differentiate themselves and respond to changing market demands.

7. Scaling the Business

Scaling a startup involves expanding its operations, increasing market reach, and optimizing processes for growth. Founders need to develop strategies for scaling that address both operational and strategic aspects. This includes scaling the team, enhancing infrastructure, and refining the business model to support larger volumes and new markets. Effective scaling requires careful planning and execution to sustain growth and maintain quality.

8. Building Strong Customer Relationships

Customer relationships are vital for a startup's success. Founders must focus on understanding customer needs, delivering exceptional experiences, and building loyalty. Engaging with customers through various channels, gathering feedback, and adapting to their preferences can drive repeat business and positive word-of-mouth. Strong customer relationships contribute to long-term success and growth.

9. Balancing Work and Well-Being

The demands of startup life can be intense, and founders often face long hours and high stress. Balancing work and personal well-being is crucial for maintaining health and sustaining productivity. Founders should prioritize self-care, set boundaries, and seek support when needed. Maintaining a healthy work-life balance helps prevent burnout and ensures sustained motivation and effectiveness.

10. Leaving a Legacy

Ultimately, many startup founders aspire to leave a lasting impact. Whether through a successful exit, a transformative product, or a positive influence on their industry, founders aim to create a legacy that extends beyond their venture. Building a startup with purpose and vision contributes to a broader legacy and inspires future entrepreneurs.

Startup founders are the driving force behind innovation and entrepreneurial success. Their journey involves turning visionary ideas into reality, overcoming challenges, and building thriving businesses. By assembling talented teams, securing funding, fostering innovation, and nurturing customer relationships, founders can navigate the complexities of startup life and achieve lasting impact. With resilience, creativity, and a clear vision, startup founders pave the way for the future of business and technology.

The Purpose of Building a Successful Online Business from Scratch

Starting an online business from scratch can be a transformative and rewarding endeavor. The purpose behind building a successful online business is not merely about financial gain but also about achieving broader goals that can impact both the entrepreneur and the market. Here's a closer look at the fundamental purposes driving this journey.

1. Realizing a Vision

At the core of any successful online business is a vision. Entrepreneurs often start with a unique idea or concept they are passionate about. This vision might involve solving a specific problem, offering a novel product, or delivering exceptional service. The purpose of starting from scratch is to bring this vision to life and make a meaningful impact in the chosen field.

2. Creating Value

One of the primary purposes of building an online business is to create value for customers. By identifying and addressing a market need, entrepreneurs can develop products or services that improve lives or solve problems. This value creation fosters customer satisfaction and loyalty, ultimately leading to a successful and sustainable business.

3. Achieving Financial Independence

Financial independence is a significant motivator for many online business founders. Building a successful online business can provide a steady income stream and offer financial stability. It also presents opportunities for scaling and generating substantial revenue, which can support personal and professional goals and provide greater control over one's financial future.

4. Leveraging Flexibility and Independence

Starting an online business offers flexibility and independence that traditional businesses may not provide. Entrepreneurs can set their own schedules, work from anywhere, and make decisions without the constraints of a physical location or traditional office environment. This flexibility allows for a better work-life balance and the freedom to pursue personal interests alongside business goals.

5. Fostering Innovation

Building an online business from scratch often involves innovation and creativity. Entrepreneurs have the opportunity to explore new technologies, develop unique solutions, and disrupt existing markets. The purpose here is to push boundaries, drive progress, and contribute to industry evolution by offering fresh perspectives and groundbreaking ideas.

6. Building a Personal Brand

A successful online business allows founders to build and enhance their personal brand. By establishing themselves as thought leaders or experts in their niche, entrepreneurs can gain recognition, credibility, and influence. This personal brand can open doors to new opportunities, such as speaking engagements, partnerships, and media appearances.

7. Contributing to the Community

Entrepreneurs often seek to make a positive impact on their community through their online businesses. This can involve supporting local causes, creating job opportunities, or engaging in ethical practices that benefit society. The purpose of contributing to the community extends beyond profit and includes fostering a positive social and economic impact.

8. Gaining Personal Growth and Development

Starting an online business from scratch is a journey of personal growth. Entrepreneurs acquire new skills, gain experience, and develop resilience through overcoming challenges. This process of learning and self-improvement contributes to personal development and prepares individuals for future ventures and opportunities.

9. Achieving Autonomy and Control

Running an online business offers a sense of autonomy and control over one's professional life. Entrepreneurs can make strategic decisions, set their own goals, and steer their business in the direction they envision. This autonomy empowers founders to shape their destiny and build a business that aligns with their values and aspirations.

10. Leaving a Legacy

Ultimately, many online business founders aim to leave a lasting legacy. Whether through a successful exit, a groundbreaking product, or a positive influence on their industry, the purpose of building a business extends beyond personal success. Entrepreneurs strive to create something meaningful that endures and inspires future generations.

Conclusion

The purpose of building a successful online business from scratch encompasses a range of aspirations, from realizing a personal vision and creating value to achieving financial independence and fostering innovation. Entrepreneurs seek to leverage flexibility, build personal brands, and contribute positively to their communities. This journey of growth, autonomy, and legacy shapes not only the business but also the lives of those who embark on it.

www.ingramcontent.com/pod-product-compliance
Lightning Source LLC
Chambersburg PA
CBHW031443210526
45464CB00005B/2312